SAMSUNG GALAXY NOTE 10 AND NOTE 10 PLUS USER'S GUIDE

The Beginner's Manual to Master Your Galaxy Note 10/10+ with Tips and Tricks

TECH REVIEWER

TABLE OF CONTENT

How to Use this Book

Welcome! Thank you for purchasing this book and for trusting us to lead you right in operating your new device. This book has covered every detail and tip you need to know about the Samsung Galaxy Note 10/ 10+ for you to get the best from the device.

To better understand how the book is structured, I will advise you read from page to page, after which you can then navigate to particular sections as well as refer to a topic individually. This book has been written in a simple form to ensure that every user understands and gets the best out of this book. The table of content is also well outlined to make it easy for you to reference topics as needed at the speed of light.

Thank you.

Other Books by the Same Author

- Fire TV Stick; 2019 Complete User Guide to Master the Fire Stick, Install Kodi and Over 100 Tips and Tricks https://amzn.to/2FnmcQ9

- Amazon Echo Dot 3rd Generation: Advanced User Guide to Master Your Device with Instructions, Tips, and Tricks https://amzn.to/31PaBTF

- Mastering your iPhone XR: iPhone XR User Guide for Beginners, New iPhone XR Users and Seniors https://amzn.to/31V4YU1

- Mastering Your iPhone XS: iPhone XS User Guide for Beginners, Seniors, and New iPhone XS Users https://amzn.to/2XizMzm

- The Beginner's Guide to Kindle Oasis 3 (10th Generation) https://amzn.to/2PwXWT7

Introduction

The Samsung brand from inception has been known to launch a new phone each year, and this keeps the Samsung fans excited as everyone is anxious to see what new features the new devices will bring.

On August 23, 2019, Samsung launched the Galaxy Note 10 and 10 plus packed with amazing features. This latest addition to the Samsung galaxy family can be said to be the best smartphone from the Samsung company so far.

The phones so alike yet have some distinct features that we will talk about in this book.

The regular Note 10 device is the cheapest of the devices launched by Samsung this year, the size of the phones is another impressive thing when you compare it with the other Note series.

In this guide, you will learn all you need to know about operating your Samsung Note 10 or 10+

explained in the simplest languages with pictures for easy understanding.

Difference Between Note 10 and Note 10+

Galaxy Note10

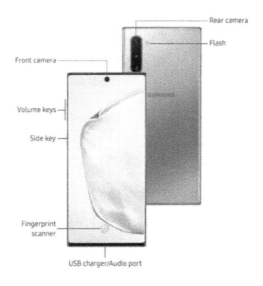

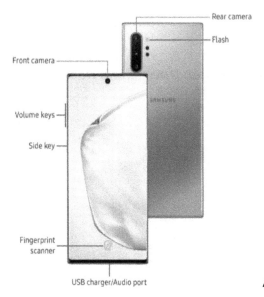

Although the two devices are very similar, we have some differences which I will highlight below.

For previous owners of the Galaxy Note 9, note 10+ is an upgrade on the Note 9, and if you are thinking of what device to get after owning a Note 9, then you should go for the Note 10+.

Galaxy Note 10 is a liter version of the Note 10+ and may not be suitable for old users who are familiar with the "S Pen." I believe that Samsung designed Note 10 to attract other android users who may not be familiar with the "S Pen" feature of the latest Samsung devices.

Screen Size and Resolution

For both devices, Samsung made use of the OLED screen that cannot be matched by other Android manufacturers. While the Note 10 comes with a 6.3 inches screen and a resolution of 1080 x 2280 (1080p), the Note 10+ comes with a 6.8 inches screen and resolution of 1440 x 3040 (1440p).

RAM and Storage

While the Note 10 comes with the 8GB RAM and 256GB storage, the 10+ comes with 12GB RAM and 256/512GB storage.

ToF 3D VGA Camera and 3D Scanner

The Note 10 comes with three rear cameras while the 10+ comes with four rear camera lenses. The rear camera lens missing in the Note 10 is the ToF (time-of-flight) 3D VGA camera that comes with an infrared light sensor.

Samsung referred to the ToF camera as a **Depth Vision** camera that owners can use to get the depth of any object in the camera frame.

Superfast Charging

The Note 10 supports the 25w fast charging while the Note 10+ supports the superfast charging at 45w. Please note that the 25W or 45W is the highest possible charging capacity for both phones.

Battery Capacity

Note 10+ is bigger than the Note 10, and it comes with a battery size of 4300 mAh while the Note 10 has a battery size of 3500 mAh. While the screen-on time of each phone will depend on how you use it and several other factors, yet, the Note 10+ battery capacity is about 22% larger than that of the Note 10.

SD Card Support

The Note 10+ supports the micro SD card while the Note 10 does not support this feature. The single SIM version of the Note 10+ has its own dedicated micro SD card slot located in the SIM card tray while the dual SIM version of the Note 10+ has a space for the micro SD card in the slot two that you can also use for with another SIM card. In the dual SIM version of the Note 10, the double slot located in the SIM card tray is only permitted to house the SIM cards. If the space in Note 10 will not be enough for you, then you may need to get the Note 10+.

Price

While the Note 10+ price starts at $1,099.99 the Note 10 price starts at $945

Chapter 1: Getting Started

Unboxing the Samsung Note 10 and Note 10+
The items in both the Note 10 and Note 10+ are the same except the phones. Below are the things you will see when you unbox your new device. Please note that this content may vary depending on your region. For instance, for some areas, Samsung does not offer a 1-to-1 exchange. However, the items listed below are included in almost all areas.

1. The Samsung Phone
2. USB connector
3. USB-C cable
4. USB-C headset
5. 25w Wall charger
6. S Pen
7. S Pen nib removal tool (tweezers)
8. S Pen spare nibs
9. Clear back cover
10. SIM card tray ejection pin
11. Screen protector

The Layout of Note 10 and 10+

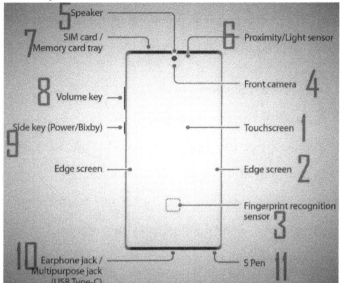

The Note 10 and 10+ come with some new features like the in-display fingerprint reader, zoom-in microphone, and the new Side key that may be confusing to even an old user of the Note series. In this part, I will explain in detail the layout of both phones, their ports, elements, and buttons, as well as how to use each of them.

1. Edge Screen

This is the curved parts on both sides of the touchscreen. Samsung included some quick tools like the edge lighting and edge panel features to the Edge Screen. I will show you how to use the Edge Screen in a later part of this guide.

2. Touch Screen

For most of the front screen of the two devices, you will notice the OLED display. It is because of this that Samsung included a plastic screen protector as most third-party screen protectors do not work with the in-display fingerprint sensor.

3. Side Key

This is the second physical button on the Note 10 and 10+. It replaced the Bixby key and can also be called the power button. With the side key, you can perform the following functions:

- Press once to turn off the screen or wake up the screen.
- Press and hold to wake Bixby.
- Press twice to launch the camera app

Of course, you can set the long press and double press to perform other functions.

Side Key Settings
By default, the side key has been customized to perform certain functions. However, you can change to your preferred shortcuts using the side key.

Double Press

With this option, you can choose what happens whenever you press the side key twice. To do this,

- Go to Settings
- Click on **Advanced Features**
- Select **Side Key**
- Click on **Double Press** to activate this feature.
- Select an option from the list below on the one you will like to access whenever you double press the side key.

- ❖ Open app
- ❖ Open Bixby
- ❖ Quick launch camera (which is the default)

Press and Hold

With this feature, you can configure the function you will like to access whenever you press and hold the side key.

- Go to Settings.
- Click on **Advanced Features**.
- Select **Side Key.**
- Under the heading for **Press and Hold,** select your preferred option:
  - Power off menu
  - Wake Bixby (which is the default option)

4. Volume Key

This key is located on the left-hand side of the phone and is one of the two keys available in the Note series. Apart from using it to control the volume, you can use the volume key to perform some other functions like:

- Zoom in/out in some apps.
- Take photos in the Camera app.
- Reboot the phone into safe mode to check whether third-party apps are responsible for the problem.
- Reboot the phone into recovery mode to clear the cache partition.
- Take a screenshot (used along with the Side key).
- Access the power menu.

The volume key has both the volume up, which is the top part of the key and the volume down key, which is the bottom part of the key.

5. Fingerprint Sensor

Both devices have the in-display fingerprint sensor, which Samsung introduced with the launch of the Note 10 and 10+. It is an exciting feature to use but also tricky if you compare it with the traditional fingerprint reader that we all know. With this new feature, you have to get familiar with the positions of the fingerprint sensor. You will see an in-depth on how to use this feature.

6. Earpiece/ Speaker

This is the part of the phone where the audio sound comes out from when on-call or playing audio.

7. Selfie Camera

With the front camera of these devices, you can take a selfie of yourself and friends.

8. Proximity/ Light Sensor

This proximity sensor feature detects that something is close to the phone. For instance, the screen goes off whenever you place the phone close to your ear to answer a call. This feature is to ensure that you do not press some buttons in error. Once you drop the phone, the screen comes on automatically.

9. USB-C Port

Samsung introduced the USB-C from the Note 7 device. In this new device, Samsung removed the headphone jack, which means that you will need to use an earphone that works with the USB-C or purchase a USB-C to 3.5mm dongle if you want to continue using your old headset. This USB-C port can be used for several functions as I will list below

- Connect your charger to the port whenever you need to charge your phone battery.
- Connect your USB-C accessories like the USB-C headsets directly to the port.
- If you want to use the Samsung DeX for PC, you can use this port to connect your phone to a windows 10 PC.

- Connect a USB connector, usually included in the box to this USB-C port, and then connect all other accessories or devices.

- While you can connect your Note 10 and 10+ to a DeX station or pad when using the Samsung DeX, you can also use this port to connect your phone to a monitor that has the DeX cable or a USB-C to HDMI dongle for same Samsung DeX.

It is, however, essential that you go for high-quality USB-C cables like the ones provided by Samsung in the box to avoid any damage to your phone.

10. SIM Card Tray

The SIM card tray in the Note 10 houses only a nano-SIM, whether it is the single or the dual SIM version. For the Note 10+, slot 1 in the SIM card tray is specifically for the SIM card, while the slot two can be used either for SIM card or SD card. But you can

11. S Pen and S Pen Slot

The S Pen is a signature for all Galaxy Note devices. Later in this guide, you will learn how to use the S Pen on your phone. Note that the S Pen for this Note 10 and 10+ usually requires approximately 10 minutes to charge because it contains an original battery, unlike Note 9 that requires just 45 seconds. To charge the S Pen, return it to the S Pen Slot.

The dimension for the S Pen slot of these two devices is different from other devices, and you must use the slot for each phone separately. Do not input the Note 10 S Pen in the slot for another device and the same for 10+.

12. Rear Camera Module

While the Note 10+ comes with four rear cameras, Note 10 comes with three rear cameras, which we have already discussed in the section that talks about the difference between the two phones.

Once you get your phone, take off the protective film from the camera lens. The camera app is configured to warn you whenever the lens of the camera is dirty.

13. Wireless Charging Coil and MST/ NFC Antenna

The phone's wireless charging coils and NFC antenna are close to the center of the phone. To use the NFC, tap the center of the phone to any NFC readers. To charge your device using the wireless charging feature, ensure to place this part close to the charging coils of the wireless charging pad (usually close to the center)

You need the MST (Magnetic Secure transmission) when you want to make use of the Samsung Pay on physical credit card terminals that will require you to swipe your card. Some thick covers or cases will not allow the wireless charging and NFC to work well. You can, however, use the Samsung official Note 10 and 10+ phone cases without encountering any issues.

14. Top Microphone

You can call this the "noise canceling" or the "secondary" microphone. When on a call, the bottom mic, by default, is used as the primary microphone while the top one is placed there to cancel noise. With the Voice Recorder app, you can assign different roles to each microphone.

15. Top and Bottom Speaker

The phone comes with two stereo speakers, one at the bottom and the other on the top.

16. Zoom-in Microphone

This microphone was newly introduced with the launch of the Note 10 and 10+ for recording video. With this microphone, sounds get automatically amplified from the objects focused on. To disable this feature, click on the icon whenever it appears. The zoom-in microphone is located close to the lens of your phone camera as it focuses on same objects as the camera lens. Several people assume that the top speaker is the zoom-in microphone.

How to Power on your device

- Press the side key and hold until the device comes on.

How to Switch off the Device

- Go to the Notification Panel at the top of the screen

- Then click on the **Power** icon.

- Select **Power off**

- A pop-up will show on the screen, click on **Power Off** again to confirm your action
- The phone will go off now.

You can also switch off your device with the steps below:

- Press both the volume down key and the side button at the same time.
- Continue to hold until you feel a vibration, and the power menu will appear on the screen.
- Select **Power off**
- Then click on **Power Off** again to confirm your action

How to Change the Power Button

You can set the side key to use for powering off your device. To activate the side button for the power-off function,

- Go to **Settings**.
- Click on **Advanced features**.

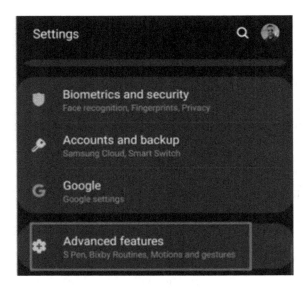

• Select **Side Key.**

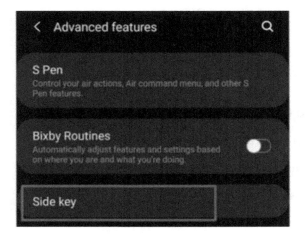

- Under the **Press and hold** option, click on the **Power Off menu.**

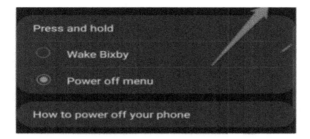

- Now you have returned the traditional power menu just by pressing and holding the side key

How to Use the Setup Wizard
When you first turn on your device, the setup wizard will guide you through the basic things you need to set up your device.

Follow the prompts on your screen to select your preferred language, choose location services, connect to a wi-fi network, learn about the features of your device, set up accounts, and lots more.

How to Name Your Device

- At the top right side of the screen, swipe down the screen to display the settings bar.
- Click on **Settings.**
- Then scroll to the last option and click on **"About Phone."**
- At the top of the screen, you will see the current name of your phone.
- Click on **Edit**, below the current phone name to change the name.
- On the pop-up on the screen, type in your preferred name, then click on **Done.**

Status Bar

The diagram below explains the status icons you will see on your device.

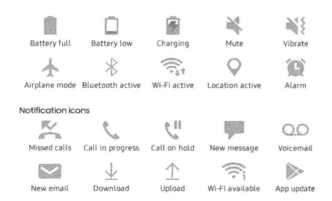

How to View the Notification panel

You can go to the notification panel from anywhere on your device. To do this,

- Swipe down from the top of the screen to display the notification panel.
- Swipe further down on the list to show the notification details and select any of the options below:

❖ Tap on an item to open it

❖ Move a notification to the right or left to clear a single notification.

❖ Click on **Clear** to clear all the notifications at once.

❖ Click on Notification settings to customize notifications.

❖ If you want to close the notification panel, click on the Back button or swipe upward on your screen.

How to Charge the Battery

The Samsung Note 10 series comes with a rechargeable battery. In the phone box, you will find the charger included for charging your phone battery. Your device and the charger may go hot while charging and then suddenly stop charging.

It is normal, and you do not need to panic. Disconnect the charger from your Samsung phone and then allow the device to cool down before you continue charging.

Show Battery Percentage on Status Bar

At the top of your phone screen, you can view the battery bar; however, you will not be able to ascertain the battery percentage of your phone except you swipe down from the top right side. Here, I will show you how to permanently set it to show the percentage level beside the battery bar.

- From the top right side of your screen, fully swipe down the notification bar.
- Click on the three dots by the top right side of the screen.
- From the pop-up, select **"Status Bar."**
- Then toggle the switch beside "**Show Battery Percentage**" to the right to enable the feature.

- The battery percentage will automatically show up beside the battery bar.

How to Access Quick Settings
From the notification panel, you can get quick access to device functions by using quick settings. Follow the steps below:

- Swipe down on your screen to reveal the notification panel.
- Further drag down the **View All** option.
- Click on a quick setting icon to enable or disable it.
- To open the settings of a "quick-setting icon," click and hold the icon.
- Click on **Search** to search your device.
- Click on **Power** to turn off the device, Restart, and options for Emergency mode.
- Click on **Settings** to give you quick access to the device's setting menu.
- To close **Quick Settings,** swipe upwards on your screen.

How to Use Wireless PowerShare

This feature allows you to charge your Samsung device using another phone. You will be unable to use some features when sharing power. Most Qi-certified devices can work with the wireless PowerShare. However, your phone battery has to be on a minimum of 30 percent to be able to share. The power efficiency and charging speed will vary with the devices you are using.

To use the wireless charging, follow the steps below:

- Go to Quick settings.
- Click on **Wireless PowerShare** and follow the instructions on your screen to use it.

- Place your phone face down and then place the compatible smartphone on the back of your Samsung Note to charge.
- You will feel a vibration or a notification sound once charging begins.
- The wireless PowerShare will automatically turn off there is no active connection within 30 seconds.
- To stop charging, move the two devices away from each other.
- To see the status of the charge, click on the notification in the notification panel.

Troubleshooting Tips when Wireless PowerShare is not working
- If you are not able to connect or you experience slow charging, remove any cover from both devices. However, you may experience slow data services or interrupted call reception when sharing power.

- Remove all covers or accessories when using this feature.

- Each device has its different placement of the wireless charging coil, move your phone until you can make a connection. Once you get the right location, you will get a notification or a vibration to alert you that the phones are connected.

- Do not use headphones when sharing wireless charging.

How to configure Supported Accessories

You can configure the accessories you intend to use on your phone from the **settings** option. Whenever you connect a new accessory to your device, you will get the opportunity to configure it. Follow the steps below to do this:

- Go to Settings.

- Click on **Advanced Features**.

- Then click on **Accessories** to activate.

How to Transfer Data to Your New Device from an Old phone

With the Smart Switch™, you can transfer music, photos, notes, messages, calendars, etc. from your old device to the new phone. Smart Switch uses Wi-fi, USB cable, or computer to transfer these items. If you do not want to install the Smart Switch app, you can make use of the On-the-go adapter included in the box to easily and quickly transfer contents. To transfer contents, follow the steps below:

- Go to the Settings option.

- Click on **Accounts and Backup.**

- Then click on **Smart Switch.**

- Follow the prompts on your screen and highlights the items you wish to transfer from the old device to the new one.

Tip: you have to set the USB option on the other device to Media device (MTP). Ensure that both devices are fully charged when transferring using a USB as the transfer can consume plenty of battery.

How to Restart your Device

- Go to the Notification Panel at the top of the screen.

- Then click on the Power icon.

- Tap **Restart.**

- A pop-up will appear on your screen, click on **Confirm** to approve your request.

- The phone will restart.

How to Restart your Device with your Voice
You need Bixby to perform this function.

- Launch Bixby and then give it a command to **"Turn off my phone"** or **"Restart my Phone."**
- Confirm your request when prompted.

How to Auto-Restart Your Smartphone
Improve your device performance by automatically restarting it at defined times. Any data that you do not save will be lost when the device restarts.

- Go to **Settings.**
- Click on **General management.**
- Select **Reset.**
- Then click on **Auto restart** and move the button to the right to enable this feature and set the parameters below:
- **Days:** choose the exact day in a week that you want the device to restart automatically.

- **Time:** select the time for the device to

  restart.

How to Unlock or Lock Your Device

Side key
Press to lock.
Press to turn on the
screen, and then
swipe the screen to
unlock it.

This

feature helps to secure your phone. By default,

once the device screen times out, it automatically

locks the phone. To lock the phone when the

screen hasn't timed out, press the side button on

the left.

47

To unlock your device, press the side key then swipe up on the screen to unlock.

How to Take a screenshot
Whenever you take a screenshot, it gets automatically saved in the screenshot album of the gallery app.

- To screenshot a view, press and hold the volume down and the power keys until you hear a click sound.

Palm Swipe to Capture A Screenshot
You can also screenshot by simply swiping the edge of your hand across the screen, from one side to the other while maintaining contact with the screen. To activate this feature,

- From the Settings tab, click on **Advanced features.**
- Select **Motions and gestures.**
- Then click on **Palm swipe to capture** and toggle the switch to the right to enable.

How to Remove the Screenshot Toolbar

Having the screenshot toolbar at the bottom of the screen can be quite irritating. Although it can be handy when you need to take a scrolling screenshot. However, it is very annoying, mainly because you have to hold on for the panel to disappear before you would be able to take another screenshot. Thankfully, Note 10 gives the option of disabling and re-enabling the screenshot toolbar. To do this,

- Go to **Settings.**
- Click on **Advanced features**
- Then click on **Screenshots and screen recorder** and move the switch to the left or right to enable or disable the screenshot toolbar

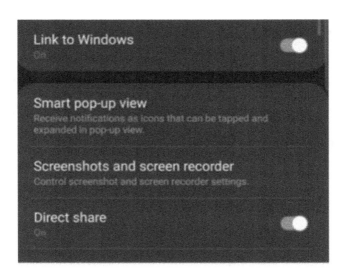

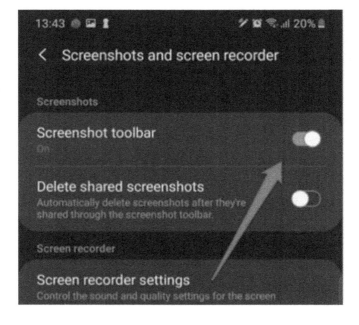

Tip: You can set your phone to automatically delete screenshots that you have shared to declutter your phone. To do this, move the switch to the right beside the **Delete Shared Screenshots** option.

How to Setup Voicemail

When you launch your phone for the first time, you can always set up Voicemail. You can also go through the phone app to access voicemail. To set up,

- On your dial key, press and hold the number 1 key.
- Follow the voice tutorial to set your password, record your name, and a welcome greeting for callers.

How to Connect to Wi-Fi

If you will rather connect to wi-fi instead of using mobile data, follow the steps below to join:

- From the settings bar, click on **Connections.**

- Then click on **Wi-fi** and toggle the button to the right to enable. And begin the search for available networks.
- Click on your desired network and enter the password, if any.

How to Manually Connect To A Wi-Fi Network
If you cannot find your wi-fi network on the list of available networks, you can manually enter the wi-fi information to connect. You will need the name of the network and its password.

- From the settings bar, click on **Connections.**
- Then click on **Wi-fi** and toggle the button to the right to enable wi-fi.
- At the end of the list, click on **Add network.**
- Input required information about the network you want to connect to. These details include: Network name as it is,

Security and password and any advanced options like proxy and IP settings.

- Click on **Save.**

How to Connect Using Wi-Fi Direct

With wi-fi direct, you can share data between two devices.

- From the settings bar, click on **Connections.**
- Then click on **Wi-fi** and toggle the button to the right to enable wi-fi.
- Next, click on **Wi-Fi Direct.**
- Select a device from the list and then follow the on-screen prompts to connect.

How to Disconnect from Wi-Fi Direct

- From the settings bar, click on **Connections.**
- Then click on **Wi-fi.**
- Next, click on a device **Wi-Fi Direct** to disconnect it.

How to Use Bluetooth

Connect your device to other Bluetooth enabled devices such as the Bluetooth headphones or even a Bluetooth enabled car infotainment system. After the devices have paired for the first time, they will automatically connect for subsequent uses without asking for a passkey.

- From the settings bar, click on **Connections.**
- Then click on **Bluetooth** and toggle the button to the right to enable Bluetooth.
- Click on the device you wish to connect to and then follow the on-screen prompts to connect.

Tip: you can also tap the Bluetooth icon from the status bar to connect to Bluetooth.

Add Dynamic Wallpapers to the Lock Screen

The Note 10 series have a new feature called the **Dynamic Lock screen** feature that rotates the artwork that displays when the screen is locked.

This feature is an excellent addition if you are one that likes changing your lock screen wallpapers. To enable this,

- Go to **Settings**.
- Click on **Lock Screen.**

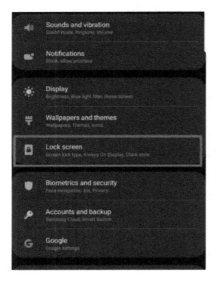

- Then select **Dynamic Lock Screen.**
- Pick a category of your choice, whether landscapes, pets, etc. and you are good to go.

How to Enable 'Lift to Wake'
You can set your device to turn on the screen whenever you lift your device.

- From the Settings tab, click on **Advanced features**
- Select **Motions and gestures**
- Then move the switch beside **Lift to wake** to enable or disable.

How to Customize Double tap to wake
Rather than using the power key, you can turn on the screen by a simple double-tap.

- From the Settings tab, click on **Advanced features.**
- Select **Motions and gestures.**
- Then click on **Double tap to wake** and enable or disable.

How to Enable Smart Stay
With the Smart stay feature, the screen will stay on whenever the front camera focuses on your face.

- From the Settings tab, click on **Advanced features.**

- Select **Motions and gestures.**

- Then click on **Smart stay** and move the slider to the right to enable or left to disable.

One-Handed Mode
This setting allows you to operate your device using one hand.

- From the Settings tab, click on **Advanced features.**

- Select **Motions and gestures**

- On the next screen, move the switch beside **'one-handed mode'** to the right to enable it.

- Then select either **Gesture or Button:**

1. **Gesture:** when this feature is enabled, you can reduce the size of the screen display by swiping up diagonally from any side of the bottom.

2. **Button:** to reduce the size of the screen, quickly tap the home three times in a row.

How to Activate Blue Light Filter

Samsung designed the blue light filter to help users sleep better, particularly if you use your phone at night. You can configure your smartphone to disable or enable this feature automatically.

- From the **Settings** tab, click on **Display.**
- Then click on the **Blue light filter** and then select from the following options:
- Move the opacity slider to set the filter's opacity.
- Click on **Turn on Now** to activate this feature.
- Click on **Turn on as scheduled** to set a time that the Blue light filter should be active.

How to Activate Night mode
When night mode is active, your device will switch to a darker theme to help your eyes adjust well at night.

- From the Settings tab, click on **Display.**
- Then click on **Night mode** and then select from the following options:
- Click on **Turn on Now** to activate Night mode.

- Click on **Turn on as scheduled** to set a schedule for night mode, either custom schedule or sunset to sunrise.

How to Turn on Adaptive Power Saving

One fantastic addition to the Note 10 series is the Adaptive Power saving mode to assist in saving power. To enable this feature,

- Swipe down from the top of the screen to access the complete quick notification panel.
- Click and hold the **Power Mode.**
- On the next screen, select the **Adaptive power-saving mode.**

How to Activate the Assistant Menu

This feature is designed for persons with motor control and other physical impairments. With the assistant menu, you can use hardware buttons and the rest of the screen by swiping or tapping. The steps below would show you how to activate this feature.

- Go to **Settings**.

- Navigate to **Accessibility** and click on it.

- Then click on **Interaction and dexterity**.

- On the next screen, enable the option for the **Assistant Menu.**

Chapter 2: Accounts and Apps

Under this option, I will show you how to set up and manage your Samsung account, Google, and email accounts.

How to Add a Google Account

To sign in to your Google account to access your cloud storage, installed apps as well as make use of your android features, follow the steps below:

- Go to Settings.
- Click on **Accounts and backup.**
- Then select **Accounts.**
- Next, select **Add Accounts.**
- On the next screen, click on **Google.**
- Input your login details or click on a new user to create a new account if you do not have an existing account or want to create a new account.
- Once you successfully login to your Google account, the factory reset protection is automatically enabled. To use FRP when you want to reset to factory

settings, you will need to input your Google account info.

How to Add Samsung Account
With your Samsung account, you have access to exclusive Samsung content. To log in, follow the steps below

- Go to Settings.
- Click on **Accounts and backup.**
- Then select **Accounts.**
- Next, select **Add Accounts.**
- On the next screen, click on **Samsung Account.**
- Input your login details or click on a new user to create a new account if you do not have an existing account or want to create a new account.

Tips to Access your Samsung Account

If you want to quickly get to your Samsung account, go from **Settings** and then click on the Samsung account.

How to Add Outlook Account

- Go to Settings.
- Click on **Accounts and backup.**
- Then select **Accounts**.
- Next, select **Add Accounts.**
- On the next screen, click on **Outlook.**
- Input your login details or click on a new user to create a new account if you do not have an existing account or want to create a new account.

App Settings

Here, you can manage the preloaded and downloaded apps.

- From the settings bar, click on **Apps.**
- Click on **Menu** to select the apps you wish to view, after which you should click on **All, Disabled, or Enabled.**

- Click on **More options** for the features below:

❖ **Sort by:** to sort apps by name, last updated, last used, or by size.

❖ **Default apps:** change or select apps that should be used by default for functions like browsing the internet or using email.

❖ **App permissions:** from here, you can set apps that should be granted permissions to use some features of your phone.

❖ **Show/Hide system apps:** to hide or show apps.

❖ **Special access:** select the apps that you want to give exclusive access permissions to functions on your phone.

❖ **Reset app preferences:** use this to return options that were changed previously.

❖ Click on an app to display and update app information. You will see the following options:

- ❖ **Uninstall/Disable:** to disable or uninstall an app. You would be unable to uninstall the preloaded apps, but you can disable them/
- ❖ **Force stop:** force an app not working to close.
- ❖ **Mobile data:** gives you information on the data used by each app.
- ❖ **Battery:** view the entire battery life spent since the last time you charged your device.
- ❖ **Storage:** shows your storage details for each app.
- ❖ **Memory:** this option would show you how memory usage.
- ❖ **Notifications:** configure how you receive notifications for each app.
- ❖ **Permissions:** to view all the permissions that each app has.
- ❖ **Set as default:** choose a particular app as a default for a specific app category like

using the Samsung browser for surfing the net.

How to Use Samsung Health

With this app, you can plan and also track the different aspects of your life that contribute to your general wellbeings like your diet, physical activities, and sleep.

- From the Apps tab, click on the **Samsung folder** and then select **Samsung Health.**

It is important to note that any information you get when using this device shouldn't be used as a diagnosis for sickness or to cure, mitigate, prevent, or treat a disease.

Several factors like environmental conditions can affect how accurate this information provided is.

Before you begin exercising, confirm from your Physician that you are fit. It is generally safe to do moderate physical exercises like brisk walking, but still, it is essential to inform your doctor especially if you have any of the conditions below:

- Asthma, Heart disease, Diabetes, Lung disease, kidney or liver disease, and Arthritis.

Samsung Notes
This app allows you to create notes that have images with footnotes, music, text, and voice recording. You can also share your notes via social network sites.

- From the Apps tab, click on the **Samsung folder**, select **Samsung Note,** and then click on **Create.**

How to Edit notes
- Launch the Samsung Notes app
- Click on a note to access it.
- Click **Edit** to make your changes
- Then click on **Save** once done.

Notes menu

Launch the Samsun Notes app and click on Menu for the options below:

- ❖ **All notes:** to view all notes.
- ❖ **Frequently used:** fast access to notes that you use regularly.
- ❖ **Shared notebooks:** access notebooks that you shared with other people.
- ❖ **Trash:** shows you all your deleted notes.
- ❖ **Categories:** Arrange notes by categories
- ❖ **Settings:** access Samsung note app settings

How to Use Split Screen

This feature allows you to use two apps at the same time. While chatting with your friends on WhatsApp, you can also be watching a YouTube video.

- Click on the **Recent menu** to access your active apps.
- Next, click on the **App icon**.
- Click on **Open in a split-screen view.**

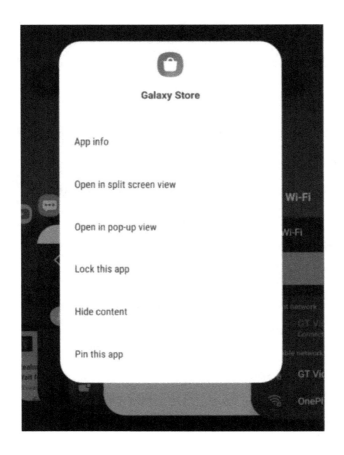

- For apps that do not have the multi-window icon, it simply means that the app does not support this feature.
- To select the second app, choose an app from the Recent menu or click on

the App List, and choose your desired
app.

- The second app world launch
  underneath the first app.

To use the Multi-window in landscape mode,
ensure to turn on Auto-rotate and turn your
phone horizontally when using a split-screen
view.

The Camera App

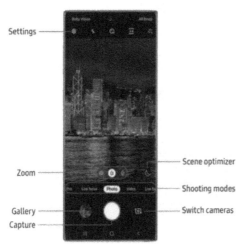

The camera
app gives you high-quality videos and pictures.

- From the app tab, click on the **Camera.**

Tip: you can access Camera by double-pressing the power key if you enabled the Quick Launch option.

How to Navigate the Camera Screen
- Once you have launched the camera, click on the screen where you want the camera focus.
- When you do this, a brightness scale will appear. Pull the light bulb to change the brightness.
- Swipe screen down or up to quickly switch between the rear and the front camera.
- Swipe your screen left or right to choose a different shooting mode.
- Click on **Settings** to access the camera settings.
- Click on **Capture** to take a picture.

Samsung Pay

With this app, you can make payments on your device. The Samsung pay is widely accepted at locations that allow you to either tap or swipe your credit card. You need to have a Samsung account to use this feature.

- From the Apps bar, click on **Samsung Pay,** then click on **Get started** and follow instructions on the screen.

Note: the system does not store your debit and credit card details on the cloud for security reasons. When using Samsung Pay on more than one device, you will need to login to each app and confirm the available payment cards.

How to Use Samsung Pay

You can use this feature by launching the app and placing your phone over the card reader for the store.

- From the Samsung Pay app, choose the card you will like to use for payments and enter your Samsung Pay PIN or scan your fingerprint to authorize the payment.

- Place your phone over the card reader for the store.
- If payment is successful, you will receive a receipt in your registered email.

Simple Pay

This app allows you access to Samsung Pay when the screen is locked, Always on Display is enabled, or from your home screen.

How to activate Simple Pay

- Launch the Samsung Pay app, click on **Menu, Settings** then click on **Favorite Cards.**
- Move the switch to the right to enable **Simple Pay** for each screen.

How to use Simple Pay

- While in any part of your phone, swipe from the bottom up.

- You will see your Simple Pay and payment card displayed on the screen.

- Pull the card down to close Simple Pay.

How to Use Samsung DeX Mode

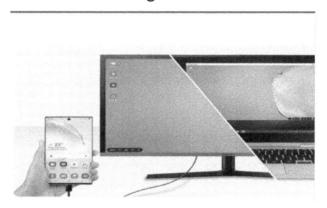

Samsung DeX is used to connect your smartphone to your computer to give you a larger screen while the mobile device can serve as a keyboard and mouse for the computer. With the Samsung Note 10 series, the DeX is now more comfortable to use. All you need is to connect your phone to Mac or Windows PC using a USB cable.

- Visit the Samsung DeX website on your Mac or PC to download and launch the installer for the Samsung DeX for PC.
- Once downloaded, connect your device to the computer using a cable.
- Once set up is done correctly, the Samsung DeX would automatically launch on your computer screen.
- From there, you can drag and drop files to your PC from your smartphone, giving you more space to manage your needed apps.
- You can still use your phone to send messages, receive calls, and also surge the net.

Home Screen Settings
These settings allow you to customize the apps and home screens.

- While on the home screen, click and hold the screen until a popup appears.
- Click on **Home screen settings** and then click on any of the options in the list as shown below to customize:
- ❖ **Home screen grid:** go through the available layouts to choose how you want your icons arranged on the home screen.
- ❖ **Home screen layout:** in this option, you can either select a single home screen that will contain all your apps or have a separate screen for apps and a different home screen.
- ❖ **Apps button:** add this button to the home screen to enable your easy access to the apps screen.
- ❖ **App screen grid:** go through the available layouts to choose how you want your icons arranged on the app screen.
- ❖ **App icon badges:** activate this feature for buttons to show on apps that have active

notifications. You can also select the style for the symbol.

❖ **Add Apps to Home Screen:** activate this feature if you want newly downloaded apps to be added by default to the home screen.

❖ **Lock Home screen layout:** activate this feature if you do not want items in the home screen to be repositioned or removed.

❖ **Rotate to landscape mode:** enable this feature if you want your device to automatically rotate when you change your device orientation to landscape from portrait.

❖ **Swipe down for notification panel:** once this feature is enabled, you can access the notification panel by swiping down from any location on the home screen.

❖ **Hide apps:** from this option, you can select apps that you wish to hide from the apps and home screen. Whenever you want to restore these hidden apps, return to this option.

❖ **About Home Screen:** click on this option to view information on your device version.

How to Unhide Apps

- Press the home screen for a while to **Display** the **Home Screen Settings**.
- Click on the **Home Screen Setting.**
- Navigate to the bottom and click on **Hide apps.**
- Click on the minus (-) sign beside apps at the top of your screen.
- Once done, click on **Apply**.

How to Enable/ Use In-Built Document Scanner

If you want to scan a document, text, or whiteboard, point your camera at the paper, and the screen would pop up with an option to scan. If you click on the scan option, you will get a very high-quality image of the scanned document. To enable this feature,

- Launch your camera app.
- Go to the camera setting at the left upper corner of your screen.
- Click on **Scene Optimizer.**
- Then activate the option for **Document scan.**

Chapter 3: Navigation bar

Recent apps ——————— Home ——————— Back

At the
bottom of your device screen, you will see the
navigation keys, as shown in the image below.

How to Activate Navigation gestures
Navigation gestures help to create more space on
your screen by hiding the navigation keys and
scrolling through the device using gestures. To

navigate your device, swipe from the bottom up on the screen.

To activate navigation gestures,

- Go to Settings.
- Click on **Display**
- Then click on the Navigation bar.
- On the next screen, select **Full-screen gestures**.
- Click on **Block gestures with S Pen** if you do not want to use S Pen for full-screen gestures.
- Click on **Gesture Hints** if you want lines to show at the bottom of your screen where you must use gestures for each navigation button.

Tip: to quickly switch between the navigation buttons and navigation gestures, make use of the quick settings menu.

How to Fix Layout of the Navigation Bar

Give your device a personal touch by changing how the Back buttons and Recent apps are displayed on the navigation bar. To set this, follow the steps below

- Go to **Settings**.
- Click on **Display**
- Then click on the **Navigation bar.**
- Under the **button order,** select your preferred layout.

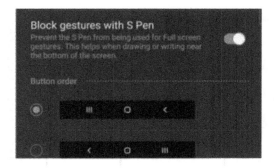

- You can also enable the **Full-Screen Gesture** that allows you to swipe up from any part of your phone to return to home screen, show recent apps or go back.

How to Configure Easy mode

Apps list

With the easy mode layout, you have larger icons and text, which will make you have a more precise visual experience. You can switch between the more straightforward design and the default screen layout.

- Go to the settings menu.
- Click on **Easy mode** to activate this feature.

- Click on **apply** to approve your selection.

How to Disable Easy Mode
- Go to **Settings**.

- Click on **Display**, then click on **easy mode**.

- Select **Standard mode**.

- Click on **Apply** to go out of the easy mode.

App Icons
From the app icons, you can launch an app from any part of the home screen.

- To add an app to your home screen, go to apps, click and hold the app icon you wish to add, then click on Add to home.

- To remove an app icon, click and hold the app from the home screen and then click on Remove from home option from the drop-down.

- Clicking on the remove an app from home will not delete the app from your phone but only remove it from the home screen.

Chapter 4: S Pen

S Pen button

How to use the new Galaxy Note 10 S Pen

The S Pen in the Note 10 and 10+ comes with some fancy features that make it look like a magic wand. Here, we will talk about all you need to know about the Note 10 and 10+ S Pen, including the new features, layout, how to customize the S Pen, and how to use these features. The S Pen, like the phone itself, is both water and dust resistant.

The Layout of the S Pen

On the body of the S Pen, you would find the following:

- **S Pen Button:** This is the button you will press to be able to access some features like Air Command, Remote control, and Airview.
- **S Pen Release Button:** To release the S Pen from the slot, push the release button inwards. To charge the S Pen, place it back into the slot.
- **S Pen Body:** the new design of the S Pen took on the unibody design. The sensors and the battery are sealed inside the body of the S Pen.
- **S Pen Tip:** You can always replace this tip. In the box, you will find the tweezers to use to replace as well as additional tips.

New Features of the Note 10 S Pen

With the Note 10 and 10+ S Pen, the Samsung company added the following:

- A 350uAh lithium-titanite battery that can last for up to 10 hours while that of Note 9 can last for less than 45 minutes.
- A 6-axis (accelerometer and gyroscope) sensor that allows the S Pen to sense both the orientation and the motion of itself.
- Because of the presence of the 6-axis sensor, you can use the S Pen for Air actions.
- It takes approximately 10 minutes to charge the S Pen fully.

How to Charge the S Pen

Return the S Pen to its slot whenever you need to charge it. Note that it takes about 10 minutes for a full charge.

Can 2 S Pen be Connected to One Device

While you can connect two S Pen to your device, however, you can only use one per time. Note 10 and 10+ have identical bodies for the S Pen, but the dimensions are different from all other models of this phone.

How to Pair Your Device with S Pen

Once you insert the S Pen into its slot, it will automatically pair with your phone. This process may take about a minute to complete.

How to Know Status of your S Pen

Whenever the S Pen is connected properly to your device, you will not see any icons related to the S Pen. However, you will see some notifications on the notification panel or status bar if there is a problem with the S Pen connection.

How to Use the S Pen Remote Functions

With the S Pen remote functions, you can remotely control some apps through the Bluetooth connection on your Galaxy note. This feature was introduced with the launch of Note 9.

To customize the double press and single press feature, go to

- Go to the **Settings** option
- Click on **Advanced Features**
- Then click on **S Pen**
- On the next screen, click on **S Pen remote** and set as desired.

How to Use Air Actions

Air Actions were introduced recently in Note 10 and 10+. This feature enables you to control some functions of supported apps by using gestures just like a magic wand. To use Air actions,

- Hover the S Pen over the phone screen.
- Tap the S Pen button
- Then swipe down/up/right-left or rotate the S Pen to access and control your desired features in apps that support the Air actions.

In the table below, I have drawn an example of how you can control the media app, camera, or gallery app by using air actions.

	Down/ Up	Right/ Left	Rotate
Media app	Volume down/ up	Play previous or go left	
Camera app	Switch camera	Previous/ next camera mode	Zoom in or out
Gallery	View	Previous	

app	details	or next items	

How to Customize Air Actions

- Go to the **Settings** option
- Click on Advanced Features
- Then click on **S Pen**
- On the next screen, click on **Air actions** and set as desired.

How to Configure Settings for S Pen

- From **Settings,** click on **Advanced Features.**
- Then click on **S Pen.**
- On the next page, you will see a list of options below. Select each one below to customize.
- ❖ **Air actions:** here, you can customize how you want the remote control to function when using an app.

❖ **Unlock with S Pen remote:** Enable this option if you want to be able to unlock your device using the S Pen.

❖ **Screen off memo:** when you activate this feature, you can create memos even when the screen is off by detaching your S Pen and writing on the screen.

❖ **Air view:** from this option, you can enable or disable the feature.

❖ **Pointer:** whenever you use the S Pen, you will see an arrow on the screen to show you available options. From this menu, you can enable or disable this feature.

How to Use Air Command

To use the Air Command option, follow the steps below:

- click on **Air command** or hold the S Pen close to your screen until you see the pointer on the screen
- then click on the S Pen button just once.

- A list will appear on your screen with the options below. Click on any of the options to perform any desired role:

- ❖ **View all notes:** use the pen to access the note app and show all your available notes. To view all the available notes, click on **Air command** then select **View All Note.**

- ❖ **Create new notes:** this is to create a new note in your note app. To create a new note, click on **Air command** then select **Create Note.**

- ❖ **Screen Write:** with this feature, you can take a screenshot and then draw or write something on the screenshot image.

- ❖ **Smart Select:** use this to draw an area then save to your gallery.

- ❖ **AR doodle:** with the AR camera feature, you can draw interactive features that follow the face movement in real-time.

- ❖ **Live message:** Use the S Pen to write or draw a short-animated message.
- ❖ **Add shortcuts:** from here, you can add additional apps to the air command.
- ❖ **Penup:** this allows you to use the S Pen to edit, color, or draw and then share with friends.
- ❖ **Translate:** hover your S Pen over a word if you want to listen to its pronunciation or see its translation.

Chapter 5: Bixby

Bixby is Samsung's virtual assistant that was created to learn and adapt to you and your needs. Bixby is built to learn what your routines are and can work with your favorite apps even to set reminders. From the Bixby home page, you will see customized contents gotten from your interactions with the virtual assistant. Bixby studies your patterns and brings up suggestions on contents that may interest you.

How to Access Bixby

You can either access the virtual assistant by pressing and holding to the Side key or just by swiping right on your home screen. Another tip to access Bixby is from the Apps list.

How to Configure Bixby Routines

From Bixby, you can get information based on your location and activity at the time or also change the settings of your device. To do this:

- Go to **Settings.**

- Click on **Advanced features.**
- Then click on **Bixby Routines.**
- Configure as desired.

Bixby Vision

Bixby works with your gallery, camera and internet apps. With Bixby, you have a deeper understanding of the things you see. Bixby helps to detect QR code, recognize landmarks, icons for translation and can even help with shopping.

Camera

You will find Bixby's vision in the camera viewfinder for clearer understanding.

- Launch the camera app
- Click on **Bixby vision**
- Then follow the on-screen prompts.

Gallery

You can use Bixby's vision on images and pictures that you have saved in the gallery app.

- Launch the Gallery app

- Click on a picture to display
- Then click on **Bixby vision**
- follow the on-screen prompts

Internet

With Bixby Vision, you can get more details about any image you see from the internet browsers.

- Launch the internet browser
- Click and hold an image, do not release until a pop-up menu appears on the screen.
- Then click on **Bixby vision**
- follow the on-screen prompts

Digital Wellbeing

With your Samsung note, you can get a daily view of the frequency you use an app, how many times you check your device, and the number of notifications that you receive. This will help you to monitor and manage your digital habits. You can also profile your device to help you shut down before you go to bed. Follow the steps below:

1. From **Settings,** click on **Digital wellbeing** and select any of the features below to view:

- **Screen time:** click on the time value shown in the dashboard circle for information on the duration each app has been active and used for that day.

- **Unlocks:** click on this to see how many times you have opened each app for that day.

- **Notifications:** click here to give you the number of notifications you received today.

- **Dashboard:** This will show you all the information contained in the features above

- **Wind down:** this setting will make your screen turn to grayscale and reduce the

number of notifications you get when you
are ready for bed.

- Notifications: This feature allows you to
customize notification settings for
individual apps.

Chapter 6: Device Security

With biometrics, you can securely log in to your accounts and even unlock your device.

Face recognition

This feature is not as secure as using PIN, pattern or password as something or someone that looks similar to your image can unlock your device.

Before you register your face, you need to check that the lens of the camera is clean and the area is well lighted then follow the steps below:

- From the Settings tab, click on **Biometrics and security.**
- Then click on **Face recognition.**
- Follow the on-screen prompts to register your face.
- You have to have enabled a PIN, pattern, or password to be able to use face recognition.

How to Customize Face Recognition

This step will show you how you can customize the face recognition.

- From the Settings tab, click on **Biometrics and security.**
- Then click on **Face recognition.**
- Click on **"Remove face data"** to delete pre-saved faces.
- Click on **Face unlock** to disable or enable face recognition.
- Click on **"Stay on Lock screen"** if you want your device to remain on the lock screen even after using face recognition until you swipe up on the screen.
- **Faster recognition:** I will advise you to turn this off for increased security and to reduce the possibility of using a similar image to unlock your device.
- **Brighten screen:** You can temporarily increase the brightness of the screen for

the device to recognize your face in dark lightings.

- **Samsung Pass:** when this feature is enabled, you can log in to your accounts online by using face recognition.

Fingerprint scanner
Rather than inputting passwords, this is an alternative security measure. With your registered fingerprint, you can log in successfully to your Samsung account. To register your Fingerprint, follow the steps below:

- From the Settings tab, click on **Biometrics and security.**
- Then click on **Fingerprints.**
- Follow the on-screen prompts to register your fingerprint.
- You have to have enabled a PIN, pattern, or password to be able to use the fingerprint for unlocking the device.

How to Customize Fingerprint Settings

Here, you can delete, add or rename fingerprints.

- From the Settings tab, click on **Biometrics and security.**
- Then click on **Fingerprints.**
- On the net screen, you will see a list of registered fingerprints at the top. To rename or remove a fingerprint, touch, and hold the desired fingerprint.
- Click on **Add fingerprints** and follow the prompts when you wish to add a new fingerprint.
- Click on **Check added fingerprints** and then scan your fingerprints to confirm if it is registered or not.

How to Enable Lockdown Mode

This feature is used to lock down your device in cases where you want no one to access your phone. If activated, this feature would disable your phone fingerprint sensor and the facial recognition scanner.

- Go to **Settings**.
- Click **on Lock Screen.**
- Navigate to **Secure Lock Settings**.
- Type in your password/Pattern/Pin.
- On the next screen, you would find the **Show Lockdown** Option and activate the feature.
- Finally, tap and hold the power button, then select **Lockdown** to enable.

Note: when the lockdown mode is enabled, it will turn off biometrics unlock, smart lock and notification on your lock screen.

Settings for Fingerprint Verification
You can use your registered fingerprint to verify your identity when logging into supported apps or actions. To do this, follow the steps below:

- From the Settings tab, click on **Biometrics and security.**
- Then click on **Fingerprints.**
- Click and enable **Fingerprint unlock** to activate unlocking your device using your fingerprint.

❖ **Samsung Pass:** when you activate this feature, you can use your fingerprint to verify when using your device

❖ **Fingerprint unlock:** Use your fingerprint for identification when opening apps that support Samsung Pay.

❖ **Faster recognition:** with this feature, you can perform fewer scans to check your fingerprints faster.

Samsung Pass
With Samsung pass, you can access your favorite services without having to input your login details for each app.

- Go to **Settings.**

- Click on **Biometrics and security.**
- Then select **Samsung Pass.**
- Log in to your Samsung account then input your biometric data.

Install Unknown Apps

The phone is built to stop the download of unknown third-party apps. However, you can bypass this setting. Before running this setting, ensure that the third-party apps are trusted.

- Go to **Settings.**
- Click on **Biometrics and security.**
- Then select **Install unknown apps**
- Click on a source or an app and then click on **Allow from this source.**

Location Services

Location services make use of the mobile network, GPS, and wi-fi to determine the device's location.

- Go to **Settings.**

- Click on **Biometrics and security.**

- Then select **Location** and move the slider to the right to enable the service.

- Click on **Improve accuracy** to use other connections below to determine your location:

❖ **Wi-Fi scanning:** Allow services and apps to automatically scan for Wi-Fi networks even when Wi-Fi is turned off.

❖ **Bluetooth scanning:** this option allows apps to automatically search for and connect to nearby devices using Bluetooth connection even when Bluetooth is not enabled

Samsung Cloud
You can back up and restore your device in the Samsung cloud.

- Go to **Settings.**

- Click on **Accounts and backup.**

- Then tap **Samsung Cloud.**

- If you are yet to add a Samsung account, you will get a guide on how to create or login to your account.
- Once you have successfully logged into your Samsung account, you can now access and manage contents saved in the cloud.

Add an Account to Backup

You can sync all your social networking, email, and video/ picture sharing accounts together.

- Go to **Settings.**
- Click on **Accounts and backup.**
- Then tap **Add account.**
- Click on one of the types of accounts.
- **Follow the** instruction on the screen to input your credentials and set up your account.
- Click on **Auto Sync Data** to activate automatic updates on your accounts.

How to Remove an Account from Your Device

- Go to **Settings.**

- Click on **Accounts and backup.**

- Tap **Accounts.**

- Then click on **Remove Account.**

Backup and Restore

You can customize your phone to back up data to

your accounts.

Backup to Samsung account

To backup using your Samsung account,

- Go to **Settings.**

- Click on **Accounts and backup.**

- Tap **Backup and restore** to get the options
  below:

- ❖ **Back up data:** Set the Samsung account to
  be used for backing up data.

- ❖ **Restore data:** restore your backed-up data
  via the Samsung account.

Backup with Google Account

To backup using your Google account,

- Go to **Settings.**
- Click on **Accounts and backup.**
- Tap **Backup and restore** to get the options below:

  ❖ **Back up my data:** this option allows the pone to back up your data and settings to the Google servers.

  ❖ **Backup account:** choose your preferred Google Account for backup.

  ❖ **Automatic restore:** activate this option for the Google servers to restore your settings automatically.

Backup to an External Storage Transfer

You can choose to use a USB storage device or an SD card to back up your data.

- Go to **Settings.**
- Click on **Accounts and backup.**
- Tap **Backup and restore.**
- Then click on **External storage transfer.**

Chapter 7: Display

Always on Display (AOD)

Whenever this feature is enabled, you can view your message alerts, missed calls, check the date and time, and also see any other preset information without having to unlock your phone. To activate, follow the steps below:

1. Go to **Settings.**
2. Click on **"Lock screen."**
3. Then tab **"Always on Display."**
4. Toggle to the right or left to enable or disable the feature. If allowing, click on the options below to customize:

- **Display Mode:** from this feature, you can set when you want the AOD to show.
- **Rotate screen:** Select whether you want the AOD in landscape or portrait mode.
- **Show music information:** enable this feature if you want to see the music details whenever you are using the FaceWidgets music controller.

- **Auto brightness:** when this feature is on, the screen will automatically adjust the brightness of the AOD.
- **About Always on Display:** to see the license and software version.

AOD Themes
To apply custom themes to the AOD, follow the steps below:

- Go to the home screen, tap and hold on the screen until a list of menus appears.
- Click on **Wallpapers** then click on AODs.
- Click on an AOD to preview and have it downloaded to the **"My Always on Displays"** list.
- Click on **View all** to see all the downloaded AODs.
- Click on the "AOD" you like then click on **"Set"** to use the desired AOD.

How to Set Screen Timeout

You can configure your screen to go off after a fixed time.

- From **Settings,** click on **Display**
- Then click on **Screen timeout**
- Then click on a time limit to set it.

Screen Resolution

You can increase the screen resolution to sharpen the quality of an image or reduce it to save battery. However, this is only available on the Note 10+. Follow the steps below:

- From **Settings,** click on **Display**
- Then click on **Screen resolution.**
- Click on your preferred resolution and then click on **Apply.**
- Some apps that do not support a lower or higher screen resolution may close when you adjust your settings.

Full Screen

You can set the apps you will like to use with the Video aspect ratio.

- From **Settings,** click on **Display**
- Then click on **Full-screen apps**
- Then click on **Apps** to activate this feature.

How to Protect Device against Accidental Touch

You can stop your screen from responding to touch whenever the device is put in a dark place like in a bag or pocket.

- From **Settings,** click on **Display**
- Then toggle the button to the right or left to enable or disable **Accidental touch protection.**

Touch sensitivity when Using Screen Protectors

- From **Settings,** click on **Display**
- Then click on **Touch sensitivity** to enable it.

How to Set Screen Saver

Set up your phone to display photos when charging or when the screen is off.

- From **Settings,** click on **Display**
- Then click on **"Screen saver"** to enable it.
- You can also configure the options shown below:
- ❖ Color: Toggle to the right to select for a change of colors per time.
- ❖ **Photo table:** activate this option if you want the pictures to show in a photo table.
- ❖ **Photo frame:** This will show the pictures in a photo frame.
- ❖ **Photo:** to pick pictures from your google photos account.
- Click on **Preview** to show you how your option will display.

How to Setup Wallpapers

Give your home screen and lock screen a unique look by using a preloaded wallpaper or favorite picture. To set up your wallpaper, follow the steps below:

- From your home screen, touch and hold the screen until a list appears on the bottom of the screen
- Click on Wallpapers.
- Click on your preferred image to select it.
- Click on the screen(s) on which you to use the wallpaper.
- Check to see if you have a Motion effect available. If available, click on it to add movement to your screens.
- Click on Set as Wallpaper, a prompt will show on the screen for you to confirm your decision.

How to Customize Themes

To apply a theme to your lock and home screens, app icons, and wallpapers, follow the steps below:

- Go to the home screen, touch, and hold your screen until a list appears at the bottom of the page.
- Click on **Themes**.
- Click on **View all** to show all the downloaded themes.
- Click on any theme to preview it and also download the theme to **My themes.**
- Click on a theme and then click on Apply to confirm your selection.

Steps to Customize Icons
- While on the home screen, touch and hold the screen.
- Click on **Wallpapers,** then click on Icons to customize.
- Click on **View all** to display all the downloaded icons on the screen.
- Click on a set of icons to preview or download to My icons.
- Click on an icon and then select Apply to confirm your chosen icon.

How to Add Widgets
Here you will see steps to add widgets to the home screen to quickly access apps or info.

- While on the home screen, click and hold the screen.
- Click on **Widgets**, then click and hold a widget, drag to your home screen before you release it.

How to Customize Widgets
After you have added a widget to your home screen, you can then customize its functions and location. To do this, follow the steps below:

- While on the home screen, click and hold a widget until an option pops up on the screen.
- From the options, you will see the following: **"Remove from Home"** to delete a widget in the home screen, **"App info"** to review widget permissions, usages and lots more, and **"Widget**

settings" to customize how the widget appears and its functions.

Gallery

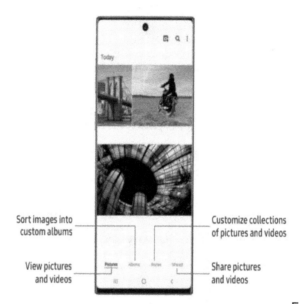

Sort images into custom albums

View pictures and videos

Customize collections of pictures and videos

Share pictures and videos

From the Apps, click on **Gallery**

View Pictures
- Launch the gallery app and click on **Pictures.**
- Click on a picture to view it. Move right or left to see other videos or photos.

- Click on **Favorite** to add that picture as a favorite.
- Click on **Bixby Vision** if you want to use **Bixby Vision** on that image.

How to Edit pictures
- Launch the gallery app and click on **Pictures.**
- Click on the picture you want to view and then click on **Edit** to show the options below:
- ❖ **Transform:** flip, Rotate, crop, or make different changes to how the picture appears.
- ❖ **Filters:** To add color effects.
- ❖ Stickers: Place animated stickers on your picture
- ❖ **Text:** Type in the text on an image.
- ❖ **Draw:** add hand-drawn or handwritten text to a picture.
- ❖ **Tone:** to modify the brightness of the image.

How to Play video

- Launch the gallery app and click on **Pictures.**

- Click on a video to view it.

- Move to the right or left for other videos.

- Click on **Favorite** to make that video a favorite.

- Click on **Play video** to watch the video recording.

How to Activate Video Enhancer

Brighten the image quality of your videos.

- Go to **Settings.**

- Click on **Advanced features.**

- Then select **"Video enhancer"** and move the slider to the right to enable.

How to Edit Video

- Launch the gallery app and click on **Pictures.**

- Click on a video to view it.

- Click on **Edit** and use the options below:

- Rotate: make the video go clockwise.
- **Trim:** if you wish to cut out parts of the video.
- **Filters:** put some visual effect touch to the video.
- **Beauty:** Improve faces in the video.
- **Caption:** input text to the videos.
- **Sticker:** place animated stickers on the video.
- **Doodle:** make a drawing on your video.
- **Speed:** Modify the rate at which the video plays.
- **Audio:** Modify the volume and input background music into the video.
- Click on **Save** and then confirm your decision when asked.

How to Create a movie
- From the gallery app, click on **Create movie.**
- Select videos and pictures you wish to add to the movie.

- Then click on **Create movie** and select an option from the list on the screen to customize your video.
- Click on **Save.**

Game Launcher
This feature automatically brings all your device games in one location. From the apps folder, click on **Game Launcher.**

Tip: if you do not see the **Game Launcher** among the list of apps, then go from Settings, click on **Advanced features,** then click on **Game Launcher.**

Edge Screen
On the edge screen, you have several edge panels that can be customized. The edge panels are used to access tasks, apps, contacts, view sports, news, and several other information.

Edge panel handle

Configure Edge panels

To customize the edge panels, follow the highlighted steps below:

- From the Edge screen, click on **Edge panel settings**.
- Move the switch to the right to enable the feature.
- You will see the following available options:
- **Checkbox:** Disable or enable individual panel.

- **Edit:** Configure each panel.
- More options:
❖ **Reorder:** Modify how the panels are ordered by pulling to the right or left.
❖ **Uninstall:** delete an Edge panel from your smartphone.
❖ **Edge Panel Handle:** Customize the style and position of the Edge panel handle.
❖ **Galaxy Store:** visit the store to download additional Edge panels.
- Click on **Back** to confirm your changes.

Edge Panel Position

You can modify how the edge panel handle is positioned.

- On the Edge screen, click on **Edge panel settings**.
- Click on **More Options**
- Then select **Edge Panel Handle** to display the following options:

❖ **Move:** pull if you want to change the location of the edge panel along the edge of your screen.

❖ **Position:** select where you want the Edge screen display should be on, whether at the left or right.

❖ **Move from any screen:** Click and hold onto the Edge panel handle to modify where its positioned from any screen.

Edge Panel Style

- On the Edge screen, click on **Edge panel settings**.

- Click on **More options**

- Then select **Edge Panel Handle** to display the following options:

❖ Color: Select your preferred color for the Edge panel handle.

❖ Transparency: Move the slider to modify the Edge panel Handle's transparency.

❖ Size: Move the slider to modify the size of the Edge panel handle.

Apps edge

Your device allows up to add as much as ten apps in 2 columns to the Apps edge panel.

- While on any screen, move the Edge panel handle to the middle of the screen.
- Swipe until you can see the Apps edge panel.
- Click on an app or app pair to access it.

How To configure Apps Edge

- While on any screen, move the Edge panel handle to the middle of the screen.
- Swipe until you can see the Apps edge panel.
- Click on **Add app** to include other apps to the Apps edge.
- On the left side of the screen, you will see available apps, click on the apps you want to add to the apps edge, and it will move to an open space on the column at the right side.

- To delete an app from the apps edge, click on **Remove.**

- To modify how the apps are arranged, move each app to your preferred location.

- If you want to make a shortcut where two apps can open in a multi-window, click on **Create app pair**

- Click on the **Back key** to save your changes.

Edge Lighting

Configure the Edge screen to light up when a notification or a call comes into the phone when the device is turned over.

- Go to **Settings.**

- Click on **Display.**

- Then select **Edge screen.**

- On the next screen, click on **Edge lighting** and move the slider to the right to enable the feature.

- Click on **Show Edge lighting,** and then select one of the following options:
- ❖ **While screen is on:** this option activates the Edge lighting feature only at the times that the screen is on.
- ❖ **While screen is off:** this option activates the Edge lighting feature only at the times that the screen is off.
- ❖ **Always:** Show Edge lighting at every time.

Edge Lighting Advanced Settings
How to customize width, color, and transparency of the Edge lighting feature.

- Go to **Settings.**
- Click on **Display.**
- Then select **Edge screen.**
- On the next screen, click on **Edge lighting** and move the slider to the right to enable the feature.
- ❖ Click on **Edge lighting style** to customize the following options:

- ❖ **Effect:** Select an effect for the edge.
- ❖ **Color:** Select custom or a preset color and activate app colors.
- ❖ **Transparency:** Move the Transparency slider to modify the Edge lighting transparency.
- ❖ **Width:** Move the Width slider to the right or left to modify the Edge lighting width.
- ❖ **Duration:** Modify how long or short you want the Edge lighting to display.
- • Click on **Done** when you finish customizing.

About Edge Screen

You can view the license information and current software version for the Edge screen feature.

- • Go to **Settings.**
- • Click on **Display.**
- • Select the **Edge screen.**
- • Then click on **About Edge screen.**

How to Record Screen Like A Pro

Write notes, record activities on your device, and use the camera to record a video overlay of yourself to share with family and friends.

- From the **Quick Settings** tab, click on the **Screen Recorder** to start recording your screen.
- Click on **Draw** to do drawings on the screen.
- Click on **Selfie Video** to use your front camera to add a recording.
- Click on **Stop** if you want to stop recording. It will automatically save in the gallery under the Screen recording album.

Settings for Screen Recorder

To control the quality and sound of your screen recorder,

- From the Settings tab, click on **Advanced features**
- Select **Screenshots and screen recorder**

- Then click on **Screen recorder settings.**

- **Sound:** to select the types of sound you want to record with the screen recorder.

- **Video Quality:** to choose the video resolution. The higher the resolution, the more memory it will need.

- **Selfie video size:** Move the slider until you get to your desired video overlay size.

How to Record Super Slow-Mo Videos

You can use your smartphone to capture action shots wherever you are. The Note 10 series can record at a real 960 frames per second with HD support. You can capture a video recording of approximately 0m4 seconds at 960 fps with about 12 secs of playback and enhance the video digitally to 960 fps with about 24 secs of playback. Follow the steps below to record a super slow-mo video.

- Launch the camera app.

- Swipe left to find the **Super Slow-Mo.**

- Set the mode to Single-take or Multi-take.
- You can enable the **Motion Detection** box to automatically record your video in Super Slow-Mo whenever an object is detected in this box.
- After the camera captures the action under the Motion detection box, the video would stop.
- When you select Super slow-mo, four options would appear on your screen.
- Click on the **Motion Detection** icon to activate it.
- With the motion detection enabled, you can edit the motion detection box to the location you want the movement to be in the shot.

Dolby Atmos for Gaming

To be able to enjoy this feature, you may need to connect a headset.

- Go to Settings.

- Click on **Sounds and vibration**

- Select **Advanced sound settings**

- Then click on **Sound quality and effect.**

- Go to the second option on the screen and move the button beside **'Dolby Atmos for gaming'** to the right to enable the feature and take your gaming experience to the next level.

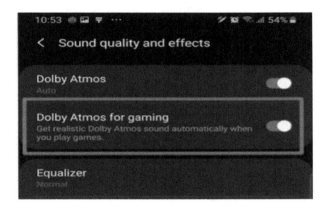

Screen mode

With the screen mode option, the screen quality is adjusted to fit different situations. Choose your preferred mode.

- From the Settings tab, click on **Display.**
- Then click on **Screen mode**
- Click on an option to choose a different screen mode.

How to Set Font size and style
Customize your device font style and size with the steps below:

- From the Settings tab, click on **Display.**
- Then click on **Font size and style** and select any of the options below
- To change the text size, move the font size slider.
- Click on **Font Style** to select a different font.
- Click on **Download fonts** to et more fonts from the Samsung store or click on a font to choose it.
- Click on **Bold font** to bolden all the fonts.

How to Set Screen zoom

Decrease or increase the size of screen contents by adjusting the zoom level.

- From the Settings tab, click on **Display.**
- Next, click on **Screen zoom**
- Then move the **Screen zoom** slider to adjust the level of zoom.

Game Booster, Block Calls/ Notifications

When playing games on your phone, you can block calls and other notifications from coming into the phone. While you enable features like Dolby Atmos and Bixby.

- Once you have launched the game, swipe from the bottom up on your screen and click on any of the options below:
- Click on **Block during games** to block features like calls or Bixby.

- Click on **Advanced Game features** to activate features like Dolby Atmos for gaming

AR Emoji

You can make an emoji of yourself to send when chatting or texting.

- From the Camera app, click on **AR Emoji** then select **Create my emoji.**
- Click on **Capture** and follow the instructions on the screen to get your emoji.

How to Record Videos

- From the camera app, move to the left or right to change to Video mode.
- Click on **Capture** to start recording your video.
- Click on **Capture** during the video recording to take a picture.

- Click on **Pause** to temporarily stop the recording and click on **Resume** to continue.
- Click on **Stop** once done with the recording.

How to Enable HDR10+ Videos

The Samsung Galaxy Note 10 series supports the HDR10+. The HDR10+ is a highly dynamic range format that gives you richer and more lively videos by optimizing contrast and color. To enable this,

- Launch the camera app.
- Go to Camera **Settings**
- Click on **Advanced Recording.**
- Then toggle the switch beside HDR10+ video to the right to enable the feature.

Note: you may not always get the same result for all the times you use this feature because it is an experimental feature.

Super Steady

With this feature, you have advanced stabilization added to your video for that smooth and professional touch. You cannot use this feature with live focus video, zoom in mic, front camera, or slow motion.

- From the camera app, swipe to set the mode to video.
- Click on **Super Steady.**
- Click on **Capture** to start recording.

Note: this can only be used in videos with 1080p in 30fps.

Zoom-in mic

Limit background noise and increase the volume of the sound you are recording as you zoom in on an audio source. You cannot use this feature with a Super steady, live focus video, or front camera.

- From the camera app, click on **Settings**

- Click on **Advanced recording options**
- Then click on the **Zoom-in mic,** move the switch to the right to enable.
- Return to the camera screen and set to Video mode
- Click on **Capture** to start recording
- Bring your two fingers together on the screen to zoom in on the audio source.

Live focus video

You cannot use this feature with Zoom in mic, zoom, or super steady.

- From the camera app, swipe to set the mode to **Live Focus video**.
- Click on a live focus effect and then move the slider to tweak the effect.
- Click on **Capture** to start recording

How to Use Edit Mode

Would you like to have a camera interface that is clutter-free? Of course, it's not all the camera modes we use daily. Most times, we find ourselves making use of the Food mode, Live Focus and Night Mode more frequently than the others. So, if you are looking for how you can declutter this camera interface, follow the steps below

- Launch the camera app
- Go to Camera **Settings**
- Click on **Camera Modes**
- On the next screen, click **On Edit Modes** then deselect all the modes you want to remove.
- You can also rearrange the placement of the different modes to suit your preference.

How to Enable Scene Optimizer

This feature is one of the recent additions to the Note series. It is an AI function as suggested by the name that helps to boost the quality of photos by studying the focused object and making appropriate changes. To enable scene optimizer, follow the steps below

- Launch the camera app
- Go to the Camera **Settings** (this is a tiny cog shaped icon located at the upper left side of the camera screen)
- On the next screen, toggle the switch beside the scene optimizer to the right to enable this feature.
- Once this feature is enabled, a blue icon would always appear on your screen when you aim your camera on an object.
- Within some tiny seconds, the camera recognizes the objects and makes the needed changes.

Tip: if you are having trouble framing your shots, enable the **Shot suggestion** menu under Camera Settings to allow AI to handle the issue with the framing.

How to Add Camera Watermark

- Launch the camera app.
- Go to Camera **Settings**.
- Navigate to the option for **Watermark,** toggle the switch to the right to enable.

Note: the watermark option would be disabled if the front camera is open as this feature only works with the rear camera.

Change Shooting Modes
The camera has several shooting modes that you can use to capture videos and pictures in specified scenarios.

- Launch the camera app, you will see the shooting modes close to the bottom of the screen, in a long row.
- Move to the left or right on your screen to change the mode.

- To see the whole list of shooting modes and their descriptions, click and hold on a shooting mode.

Chapter 8: Calls and Messages

Messages

You can share emojis, photos, or even say Hi to friends using the messaging app.

To compose a message, go to Apps

- Click on **Messages**
- Then select **Compose.**

Message search

Use the search button to find a message faster,

- Launch the Message app and click on **Search.**

- Input a keyword into the search field and then click on Search.

How to Delete Conversations

You can delete conversation history that you no longer want on your device.

- From the Message app, click on **More options**

- Then select **Delete** and click on the conversations you wish to delete.

- Click on **Delete** and confirm your action when prompted.

How to Setup Emergency Alerts

Emergency alerts warn you against dangers and other situations at no charge.

- From Messages, click on **More options**
- Select **Settings**.
- Click on **Emergency alert settings** to modify notifications for emergency alerts.

Send SOS messages
You can reach out to the desired contact when in an emergency through text messages.

To set up this feature,

- Go to **Settings**
- Click on **Advanced features**
- Select **Send SOS messages** and then move the slider to the right to enable this feature.
- Click on **Send messages to** and include recipients either by choosing from your contacts or by creating new recipients.
- To add a picture using the rear and front camera, click on **Attach pictures.**
- Click on **Attach audio recording** to add a 5-sec audio recording in your message.

- Tap the power key in quick succession three times to send the SOS message.

Message Settings
To customize your settings for multimedia and text messages.

- From Messages, click on **More options**
- Then select **Settings.**

How to Add a Contacts
From the Apps menu, click on **Contacts** then click on **Create contact.**

How to Edit a Contact
- From contacts, click on the name of an existing contact.
- Select **Edit.**
- Click on the field you wish to change, add, or delete details.
- Click on **Save.**

How to Message or Call a Contact

- From contacts, click on the name of an existing contact.
- Click on **Message** or **Call.**

How to Favorite a Contact

- From contacts, click on the name of an existing contact.
- Click on **Add to Favorites** to include the contact as a favorite.

How to Share a Contact

- From contacts, click on the name of an existing contact.
- Click on **Share.**
- Select either Text or vCard file (VCF)
- Pick the method you wish to share through and follow the on-screen guide.

Tip: click on QR code when viewing a contact to share the details with friends.

How to Enable Direct share

This feature will allow you to share things with your contacts from any app.

- Go to Settings
- Click on **Advanced features.**
- Then click on **Direct share** and toggle switch to the right to enable.

How to Create Groups

- From **Contacts,** click on **Menu**
- Select **Groups**
- Then click on **Create group** and click on individual fields to input group details like group name, ringtone, and to add a member.
- Click on **Save.**

Add or Remove Group Contacts

- From **Contacts,** click on **Menu**
- Select **Groups**
- Then click on a group.

- Touch and hold a contact you want to remove, then click on **Delete.**
- To add a new contact to a group, click on **More options> Edit group > Add member**
- Click on the contact you want to add.
- Click on **Done**
- Then click on **Save.**

How to Import Contacts
- From **Contacts,** click on **Menu.**
- Then select **Manage contacts.**
- Click on **Import/export contacts.**
- Next, click on **Import** and follow the instruction on the screen.

How to Export Contacts
- From **Contacts,** click on **Menu.**
- Then select **Manage contacts.**
- Click on **Import/export contacts.**
- Next, click on **Export** and follow the instruction on the screen.

Phone App

With your Phone app, you can do more than just making calls.

- Click on the **Phone icon** from the Home screen.

How to Make a Call
- Click on the phone icon
- Type in the number using the keypad
- Then click on **Call** to begin the call.

Enable Swipe to Call

You can call a number or contact by swiping the number to the right. To enable this feature,

- Go to Settings.
- Click on **Advanced features**
- Select **Motions and gestures**
- Then click on **Swipe to call or send messages** and move the slider to the right to enable this feature.

Make a Call from Recent Tab

The call log records all your outgoing, incoming, and missed calls.

- From Phone, click on **Recents** at the top of the screen to show a list of recent calls.
- Click on a contact, and then click **Call**.

Make a Call from Contacts

- Launch the contacts app, then swipe your finger to the right of the desired contact to call that number.

How to Answer a Call

Whenever you receive a call, your phone will ring, and you will see the caller's name and phone number on the screen. Move the **Answer slide** to the right to attend to the call.

Tip: You can also click on **"Answer" o**n the incoming call pop-up screen to answer the call.

How to Decline a Call

Move the **Decline slide** to the left to reject a call and have it sent to your recorded voicemail.

Tip: You can also click on **"Decline" o**n the incoming call pop-up screen to reject the call.

Decline a Call with a Message
On the incoming call screen, pull the Send

message button upward and choose a message.

Tip: You can also click on **Send Message o**n the

incoming call pop-up screen and select a

message.

End a Call
Click the end button once done with the call.

Multitask while on a Call
While on a call, you can switch to speaker or

headset, increase call volume, and perform other

multitasking functions.

- Press the Volume down key to decrease
  and volume up to increase call volume.
- Click on Bluetooth to continue the call
  using a Bluetooth headset.
- Click on **Speaker** to continue the call via
  the speaker.
- You can exit the call screen while on a call
  to use another app.

- When ready to return to the call screen, pull the status bar down and click on the call in the notification panel.
- To end a call while off the call screen, pull down the status bar and click on the red end call button.

Source Contacts from Places
You can search for nearby venues and businesses for their contact details and directions.

- On the phone screen, click on **Places.**
- Click on a category to search nearby.
- Then click on the desired location to view contact details and directions.
- You have to enable location services to enjoy this feature.

Access Call log
- From Phone, click on **Recents** at the top of the screen to show a list of recent calls.

How to Save a Contact from A Recent Call

- From Phone, click on **Recents** at the top of the screen to show a list of recent calls.
- Click on the call that has the details you want to add to your contacts.
- Then click on **Add to contacts**
- Click on **Update existing** or **Create contact.**

How to Delete Call Records

- From Phone, click on **Recents** at the top of the screen to show a list of recent calls.
- Hold on the call you wish to remove from the call history.
- Click on **Delete.**

How to Block a Number

When you block a number, every attempt from that number to reach, you will go straight to voicemail; however, you will not receive the messages.

- From Phone, click on **Recents** at the top of the screen to show a list of recent calls.
- Click on the number you wish to block.
- Click on **Details,** then select **Block**, and confirm once prompted.

To modify your Blocked contacts from settings,

- Click on **More options** from the phone screen.
- Select **Settings**
- And then click on **Block numbers.**

Speed dial
- Click on **Keypads** from the phone screen.
- Click on **More options**
- Then select **Speed dial numbers.**
- On the next screen, you will see available speed dial numbers.
- Number one is automatically reserved for voicemail.

- Click on an unassigned number.

- Click on **Menu** if you want to choose a different speed dial number from the one in sequence.

- Click on **Add from contact** or type in a number or name to assign a speed dial number to your contact.

- You will see the selected contact shown in the speed dial number box.

Make a call with Speed dial

- From the phone screen, click and hold the speed dial number for the contact you want to call.

- If the digits for the speed dial number is more than one, type the first digit while you hold the last digit.

Remove a Speed dial number

You can remove a number from your speed dial

- Click on **Keypads** from the phone screen.

- Click on **More options**

- Then select **Speed dial numbers.**
- On the next screen, you will see available speed dial numbers.
- Click on **Remove** beside the contact you want to delete.

Make Emergency Calls on Lock Screen
Regardless of whether the phone is locked or not, you can always call the emergency phone numbers for your region.

- From the phone screen, type in the emergency telephone number (911 if in the USA)
- Then click on **Call.**
- When your phone is locked, you can only access the emergency contacts while the other details on the phone stay secure.

Phone settings
Change phone apps settings here.

- Click on **More options** from the phone screen.
- Then select **Settings.**

Place a Multi-Party Call

If your mobile service provider offers this feature, you can initiate another call while on an existing call.

- While on the active call screen, click on **Add call** to begin dial the second number.
- Type in the new number and click on **Call.**
- Once the receiver picks, click on **Merge** for a conference call where you can hear the two parties at the same time.

TTY Mode

TTY (teletypewriter) is a telecommunications device used by people who are hard of hearing, deaf, or have some language or speech disabilities to communicate via the telephone.

- From Phone, click on **More options.**

- Then select **Settings**

- Click on **Other call settings**

- On the next screen, click on **TTY mode.**

- Click on TTY Full, TTY Off, TTY VCO, or TTY HCO.

Chapter 9: Troubleshooting

In this chapter, we will discuss how to troubleshoot your device, from resets to checking for software updates, and so on.

Software Update

You can check and also install available updates on your mobile phone.

- Go to Settings.
- Click on **Software update** to display the options below:
- ❖ **Download and install:** check for updates for system software and install available ones.
- ❖ **Last update:** For details on when the current software was last updated.

How to Reset your Device

When you perform a factory reset on your device, it resets the phone to its original form without touching the account settings, language, and security. The reset does not also affect your data.

- Go to **Settings.**
- Click on **General management.**
- Select **Reset.**
- Then click on **Reset settings**
- Click on **Reset settings,** and confirm your decision when prompted.

How to Reset Network Settings
You can reset Bluetooth, mobile data, and Wi-Fi settings with the Reset network settings.

- Go to **Settings.**
- Click on **General management.**
- Select **Reset.**
- Then click on **Reset network settings**
- Click on **Reset settings,** and confirm your decision when prompted.

How to Reset Accessibility Settings
Follow the steps below to reset settings for device accessibility. The reset will not affect your data.

- Go to **Settings.**

- Click on **General management.**

- Select **Reset.**

- Then click on **Reset accessibility settings**

- Click on **Reset settings,** and confirm your decision when prompted.

How to Perform Factory Data Reset

Resetting your device to factory default will wipe off all the data you have in your device permanently, including downloaded applications, account settings, system and application settings, data, videos, photos, music, and all other files apart from documents stored on an external SD card.

Before you reset your device, confirm that you have transferred all the information you do not want to lose.

Also, log in to your Google account and confirm you know your login details as the reset will also wipe off your Google account, and you will need to log in again after the reset to be able to access the Google account.

To reset your device:

- Go to **Settings.**
- Click on **General management.**
- Select **Reset.**
- Then click on the **Factory data reset.**
- Next, click on **Reset** and follow the instructions on the screen to carry out a reset.
- Once the device comes back up, follow the instructions on the screen to set up your device.

Factory Reset Protection
Factory Reset Protection is automatically activated on your device when you first log in to a Google Account. With the FRP, other people will be unable to use your device if they perform a factory reset without your knowledge. Once you perform the factory reset on that device, the user

will then need to input your login credentials to be able to use the device again. Should you need to send your device to a Samsung authorized service center, ensure to delete your Google account and then perform a factory data reset.

How to Enable Factory Reset Protection
Once you successfully login to a Google account on your device, it will activate the FRP feature.

How to Disable Factory Reset Protection
To disable this feature from your device, delete all Google accounts from your phone.

- Go to **Settings.**
- Click on **Accounts and backup.**
- Select **Accounts** and click on your **Google account.**
- Then click on the **Remove account.**

How to Enable Find My Mobile
With this feature, you can protect your device from theft or loss by configuring the device to be tracked online, locked, or for data on your device

to be remotely deleted from the device. You need to have a Samsung account and also enable the Google location service to use this service.

- Go to Settings
- Click on **Biometrics and security.**
- Then click on **Find My Mobile** and move the slider to the right to enable this feature.
- Enable the following features:
- ❖ **Remote unlock:** this option allows Samsung to store your pattern, PIN, or password, which you can use to control and unlock your phone remotely.
- ❖ **Send the last location:** This option alerts your phone to send its last location to the **Find My Mobile** server when the battery charge goes below a specified level.

How to Activate Screen Reader
This feature allows you to navigate your screen without seeing the screen.

- Go to **Settings.**

- Click on **Accessibility.**

- Then select **Screen reader** and click on any of the options below:

❖ **Voice assistant:** Receive audio feedback when operating your device like what you select, touch, or activate.

❖ **Tutorial:** for a guide on using the Voice assistant.

❖ **Settings:** Customize the Voice assistant to suit your needs.

Sounds and Hearing Aids
You can modify the quality of audio when using earphones or hearing aids.

- Go to **Settings.**

- Click on **Accessibility.**

- Then select **Hearing enhancements** and click on any of the options below:

❖ **Sound detectors:** with this option enabled, you will get alerted if the doorbell rings or the phone detects a crying baby

❖ **Mute all sounds:** Disable all audio and notifications for privacy.

❖ **Hearing aid support:** Improve the quality of sound for better use with hearing

❖ aids.

❖ **Left/right sound balance:** Move the slider to the left or right to adjust balance when playing audio in stereo.

❖ **Mono audio:** move to mono audio from the studio when using a single earphone.

Dual Messenger

The dual messenger allows you to have two accounts for a single app.

- Go to **Settings.**
- Click on **Advanced features**
- Then select **Dual Messenger.**

- Move the slider to the right beside each supported apps to create a second account for the apps.
- If you want to be able to choose the contacts that can access the secondary messenger app, click on **Use separate contacts list.**

Navigation Tips

When operating a touch screen device, the best is to lightly touch the pad on your finger or a designed pen on the screen. If you use excessive force or a metal object not approved on your touch screen, it may cause the glass screen to damage and void any warranty available on the device.

Tap Tips

- To launch or select an item, lightly touch the items.
- Click on an item to select it.

- Double click on an image to either zoom out or zoom in.

Swipe Tips

- Gently drag your fingers across the screen to make a swiping gesture.
- To unlock your phone, swipe from the bottom of the screen upwards
- To scroll through the menu options or home screens, swipe your screen.

Tips to Drag and drop

- This feature allows you to click on an item and hold the item to move it to a new location.
- Hold and drag an app shortcut to move and drop it on the Home screen
- Drag a widget you wish to move to a new location.

Touch and Hold

- For items you want to activate, touch and hold.
- To display pop-up menu options of an item, touch, and hold.

- Touch and hold your home screen to allow you to customize the screen.

Zoom In And Out

- Bring both the forefinger and the thumb together or space them apart to either zoom in or zoom out, respectively.
- To zoom out, move your forefinger and thumb together on the screen.
- Space your forefinger and thumb on the screen to zoom in.

CHAPTER 10: Conclusion

Now that you have known all there is to know about the Samsung Galaxy Note 10 and 10+, I am confident that you will enjoy operating your device.

These latest additions to the Samsung family have helped to make things easy and reduce stress only if you have the right knowledge and know-how to apply it, which I have outlined in this book.

All relevant areas concerning the usage of the Galaxy Note from taking out of the box to set up and operations are outlined and discussed in detail to make users more familiar with its operations as well as other information not contained elsewhere.

If you are pleased with the content of this book, don't forget to recommend this book to a friend.

Thank you.